DIARIES
of a
VISIONARY
Inspiring Dreams

DESIRI OKOBIA

DOV PUBLISHING HOUSE

This book is dedicated to my family:

My father,

you taught me how to chase my dreams.

My mother,

you taught me to never settle for less than the best.

My brothers,

I pray that one day we will all make heaven our home.

My sister,

may we continue to walk this journey of salvation together.

Amen.

Acknowledgements

I acknowledge that this is a divinely inspired piece of work. Thank you Heavenly Father for laying creativity and inspiration at my finger-tips. I also thank my Pastor for your ministry and timely sermons over the years. May the Lord's favour continue to rest upon you!

Table of Contents

Foreword

It is one thing to go through something, but it is another thing entirely not only to write about it, but to be willing to share it with others. With her book, 'Diaries of a Visionary – Inspiring Dreams,' Desiri Okobia does just that. She invites us into her world as she shares her testimonies and experiences.

She shares some insightful wisdom and lessons that she has learnt as she has travelled the path that God has placed her on, her journey certainly hasn't been an easy one, yet she is not afraid to share this with her readers.

She challenges us to trust God, look to him for guidance and to apply biblical truths to what we are going through. It is refreshing to read such honesty as she shares the experiences that she has gone through and how God has worked through her and in her.

You may as you read through this book find that your own experiences are similar to hers, and as you begin to relate to her testimony and story you will also find wisdom and advice that is just as applicable as it is insightful.

I encourage you to read each page with an open heart and allow the Holy Spirit to minister to you as she shares with you the lessons that she learnt and provides much needed advice and guidance.

— **Ps. Leighton Ainsworth**
Pastor, Potters House Christian Fellowship,
London, UK

Introduction

'Diaries of a Visionary' started off as a thought, the thought became a blog and the blog transpired into a book – a collection of bestsellers!

This is my diary, full of my precious thoughts and revelations about God. I wrote this book to share my story and to encourage and empower my readers on this journey called life. Sometimes as writers we have to metaphorically cut ourselves open and bleed onto the pages – follow my journey. I may not know your story but I know that God has great plans for your life. I have proof of this!

> **Jeremiah 29:11** *"For I know the thoughts that I think toward you, says the LORD, thoughts of peace and not of evil, to give you a future and a hope."*

I hope that my testimony inspires you. I pray that you are enlightened as I share my thoughts, my journey and the things that Jesus taught me.

CHAPTER 1

My Journey

Dear Diary,

L et me start by telling you the story of how I came to Christ.

Whilst I was growing up I was usually the quiet girl in the classroom, when all of the other children were outside playing I was the one inside the classroom reading books. Eventually I discovered a love for subjects like dance and drama. I enjoyed these activities because they allowed me to express myself in a creative way. I was quiet in class but once I hit that stage I became a completely different person. I remember my first time dancing on stage, I was at secondary school; I was 11 years old and I performed a street dance routine in the school talent show. My classmates were astonished to see me up there dancing on stage; no one knew that I had it in me. I was awarded third place in that talent show and I was very proud of myself. The stage became my platform, a place where I could escape from all of my inhibitions.

My passion for the performing arts continued to increase and I began attending theatre school in the evenings and at weekends. As time went on, I found myself falling more and more in love with the theatre world, I wanted to make a career out of it. Growing up with Nigerian parents I knew that it would not be realistic for me to pursue a full time acting career. It had been instilled in me to finish school and choose a stable career.

After secondary school, I attended Kings College University of London to study for a degree in Law. In 2006, I graduated from university and I decided that it was time for me to follow my dreams.

American Dream

I made plans to move to America and pursue my career as an actress in Hollywood. By this time I had built up my acting portfolio by attending theatre school in London, taking part in theatre productions and appearing in some TV shows. I felt that there would be more opportunities for me in America. I didn't know anyone in Los Angeles so I decided to stop in New York first. I had some family friends living in the outskirts of New York, in Yonkers, so I stayed there for a while and commuted to Manhattan. New York is similar to London, and I was used to the city life. I had it all planned out: first New York, and then eventually I would move to LA and work as an actress, live in a nice house on the beach and drive a red convertible. Yep! That's all I wanted to do. I thought that once I made it to Hollywood, my life would be complete! I was looking for purpose.

New York New York!

Eventually I moved to the Bronx, New York and rented a room in an apartment near Yankee stadium. This was more convenient for me as it was easier for me to commute to Manhattan. During the daytime I would go to auditions and casting calls for modelling jobs, music videos and acting work. In New York everyone wanted to be a model or singer or some kind of entertainer. Most evenings I would go out to clubs and industry events to network and find out about other auditions and casting calls. I also got a part-time job working behind the bar in a soul food restaurant in Harlem. In my spare time, I worked as a promotional model, mainly promoting alcoholic beverages because they paid $25 per hour. Financially, I was pretty much set. I had enough money to pay my rent and bills and time to look for auditions and castings. The New York hustle was real!

It's so easy to get caught up in the twenty – four hour lifestyle, and New York really is the city that doesn't sleep. Before I knew it, I was not only attending industry events, but going out in the evening just became a lifestyle. Sometimes I would take part in fashion shows and music videos, other nights I would just go out with friends and people that I met during my castings and auditions. New York was only supposed to be a stop-gap, eventually my plan was to move to LA as there were more acting opportunities available. New York seemed more lucrative for people trying to make it as singers and rappers as opposed to actors.

Things were getting a bit quiet in New York so I decided to do some studying. I found an 8 – week course that I could enrol on in order to study for the New York Bar exam. This was not in my original plan but I decided to go for it, an extra qualification wouldn't hurt. I thought that since I was living in New York meeting all of these industry people maybe I could be an Entertainment Lawyer. At least my time in New York wouldn't be a complete waste of time. If only it were that simple! I passed the Bar but I didn't actually have a green card, and I was only there on a holiday visa.

The Hair Salon

In February 2007, I was at a hair salon in Manhattan, preparing my hair for a hair modelling show. The salon was full of Christian literature as well as hair magazines. To my surprise, the salon owner was a devoted Christian. His name was John Anderson, and while I was getting my hair done John asked me whether or not I was a Christian. He wanted to know whether I believed in God. I told him that I was a Christian, and that I did believe in God. He then asked me whether I was born again. At the time I didn't really know what it meant to be born again. I just thought that it was a denomination, you know, the Catholics, the born-again? I didn't actually know what he meant.

This was when he told me about Jesus Christ and how he died on a cross for our sins: *"For God so loved the world that He gave His only begotten Son, that whoever believes in Him should not perish but have everlasting life."* (John 3:16) To be born again means to turn from your sins, ask for forgiveness and accept Jesus Christ as your Lord and Saviour: *"Most assuredly I say to you, unless one is born again he cannot see the kingdom of God."* (John 3:3).

I believed in Jesus Christ but I had not accepted Him as my Lord and Saviour. I didn't read the bible; I didn't pray; I didn't even go to church on Sunday to listen to God's Word. God was so gracious that even the midst of this He still found a way to reach out to me. John asked me if I wanted him to lead me in a prayer, he said that if I wanted to accept Jesus Christ into my life then he would lead me in a sinner's prayer. I readily accepted, I had heard the stories about Jesus Christ on the cross, I had seen the Christmas plays but I had never actually taken the step of entering into a personal relationship with Him. John asked his colleague Richard to join with us in this prayer. I remember them quoting Matthew 18:20: *"for where two or three are gathered in my name, I am there in the midst of them"*. This meant that Jesus was in our midst.

We went to the back of the salon and they led me in a sinner's prayer. That day I asked Jesus Christ to come into my life. I felt so rejuvenated after this prayer, little did I know that my whole life was about to change. Although I didn't fully understand everything that there was to know about Jesus Christ and how to live for Him, I knew that I had embarked on a new journey. John Anderson said that this was my new birthday and that I should ask God for whatever I wanted, me in my ignorant state asked for a job in a bar because I wanted to make more money on tips. They allowed me to pray for the job and I didn't see the problem. I knew that I wouldn't be tempted to drink I just wanted to work in a bar and make money. John and Richard invited me to their church so that I could continue to grow in my faith.

Brooklyn Life

Shortly after this day I ended up getting a job in a bar in downtown Brooklyn. This was so dangerous, working in a bar in Brooklyn then travelling home by metro back to the Bronx. Looking back now, I don't know what I was thinking. God must have assigned angels to watch over me. I was supposed to attend church with John and Richard but I didn't get around to it. I was so busy working in the bar and attending castings from time to time that I didn't even get around to attending the church services. At this point I was still so consumed in my New York life. Things were going ok.

In the summer of 2007, I spent a couple of weeks in Los Angeles where I took part in a short film playing an apprentice witch. Random, I know!

When I got back to New York I managed to secure an acting agent who agreed to sponsor me for a work visa so that I could stay in New York for longer instead of travelling back to London every few months. I originally travelled to New York on a holiday visa so I had to return to London every 3 months in order to renew the 90 day time limit. My plan was to go back to London and come back on a 6 month visa so that I would only have to travel once or twice a year. It was getting expensive. I don't know where I got the money to keep travelling back and forth to New York every 3 months.

Family Ties

It just so happened that when I prayed for salvation in the hairdressers in February 2007, my older brother, who was living in London at the time decided to give his life to Jesus Christ as well. It was just a coincidence that this happened, I found out via an email conversation with him. So anyways, when I went back to London for one of my short 2 week visits he invited me to his church. I think I visited his church one time in the summer of 2007 during one of my short visits before going back to New York. Little did I know that his church was soon going to become mine as well. God, the Master Orchestrator!

Whilst I was in London during November 2007 I attended the US embassy to apply for a 6 month visa. This process took longer than expected so I ended up staying in London for longer than my usual two weeks and attending my brother's church. This was one of the first times I had actually sat down in a church service since praying in the hair salon in New York in February of that year. I remember the pastor saying at the end of the sermon: "Are you ready to meet your Maker? If you were to die right now and stand before God are you ready?" That's when it hit me, I couldn't even bow my head that day I was literally just looking up at the preacher. I had never felt so far away from God as I did at that moment – am I ready to meet my Maker? No!

This was a serious reality check, the light switched on. What was my life about? I have come to London to get my visa to go back to New York so that I can work in a bar in Harlem and pursue my dreams of becoming an actress in Hollywood. I had no relationship with God or any knowledge of His plans for my life. Am I ready to meet my Maker?

Take me to the King

That day I answered the altar call I prayed and gave my life to Jesus Christ! This time I didn't just pray and go back to my old life, well my old life was in New York so I couldn't go back just yet anyway. I stayed in London for a few months and continued going to church, I started praying and reading my bible regularly. The bible says that *"Faith comes by hearing,"* (Romans 10:17) and it really does because the more that I continued to attend the church the stronger I became in Christ. I began to pray and ask God to help me let go of my will and seek His will for my life! One of the scriptures that really helped me was, *"Do not love the world or the things in the world. If anyone loves the world, the love of the Father is not in him. For all that is in the world – the lust of the flesh, the lust of the eyes, and the pride of life - is not of the Father but is of the world,"* (1 John 2:15 -16).

The things that were drawing me into the world were not of God. I meditated on this scripture day and night and night and day. That was one of my greatest struggles in coming to Christ – letting go of my will. I just wanted the things of the world. My view of success was the lights, the camera and the Hollywood life. Hollywood is just an illusion. These were the ideas that consumed my life, don't get me wrong there is nothing wrong with having goals and ambitions, but when they take the place of God in your life then there is a problem.

When the devil tried to tempt Jesus in Matthew 4 he said: *"I will give you all the kingdoms of the world if you fall down and worship me,"* but Jesus replied, *"Away with you Satan! For it is written, You shall worship the Lord your God and Him only you shall serve."*

Anything that takes the place of God in your life is an idol. I really had to ask God to set me free from every idol and enable me to seek His perfect will for my life. God is so faithful.

Journey to Redemption

"Good things come from above and not from abroad"

In January 2008 I went back to New York with a different mindset, ok I'm still going to live here but I'm going to find a church to attend, give up my job in the bar and just do regular promotional model jobs that don't involve promoting alcohol. So I started attending the New York branch of my London church. I invited my house mate and a couple of my friends to attend the church – things seemed to be going well. I'm saved now and I'm living in New York City. But again, God the Master Orchestrator had already set his plan for my life in motion. I attended the church in New York for a few months whilst I was in New York and then I went back to London.

In May 2008 I got baptised, I invited my sister to my baptism and then she ended up praying to give her life to Jesus Christ as well. I still remember the lyrics to my baptism song 'Goodbye world, I stay no longer with you, goodbye pleasures of sin, I stay no longer with you I've made up my mind to go Gods way the rest of my life.'

At this point I had not fully committed to moving back to London but I was committed to serving God. I was praying and actively seeking the will of God for my life. In May 2008 I was at a bible conference in London and God spoke to me so clearly through one of the sermons. As I was deliberating about whether to stay in New York or move back to London I remember the preacher saying: "Good things come from above and not from abroad."

This was a Word for me, time to go home. I still had plenty of my belongings in my room, in my apartment in New York so whatever the case was I still had to go back to New York one last time.

Between the Nations

It's June 2008. I'm back in New York. It's a Sunday afternoon.

I attended my church in the Bronx as usual. This particular afternoon the Pastor, his name was Pastor Robert, decided to ask me what I was doing going back and forth between the nations. He said, "I believe that you're saved but you still want to be in the driving seat of your life, when you get saved you have to let God be in the driving seat you have to sit in the passenger seat." He told me to go home pray and ask God where He wants me to be. I have come to realise, the will of God has a location! I remember asking Pastor Robert, how I will know that it's Gods voice that I am hearing and not my own. He said usually when he wants to do something he finds that what God is telling him is the opposite of what he wants to do. He said that I should go home and pray about this situation and he guarantees that God will give me an answer. So I went home knelt

24

on the floor beside my bed and prayed. "Ok God so where do you want me to be?" I felt a peace and I got a clear answer.

When I got back to church the following week, I told Pastor Robert that I had prayed about this and that I was moving back to London. He asked me whether I was happy with that decision I said "no", but did I have peace with that decision I said "yes!" There was my answer, when you are in the will of God there is perfect peace.

Home Time

Ok, so this is my last month in New York. I remember one particular night that I came home late and there were a bunch of guys outside my apartment. As I walked past them I smiled and nodded and quickly went inside. Shortly after I got inside my apartment, a guy that had come to visit my housemate left to go home and the same guys that were outside of the apartment attacked and robbed him. These were the same guys who I had just walked past less than an hour beforehand. That day my eyes were truly opened to the grace of God upon my life. All those times that I was taking late night train rides from Brooklyn to the Bronx and not one time had anyone tried to attack me. The Bronx is actually supposed to be the most dangerous part of New York but I didn't actually experience any of that danger. Somehow God had shielded me from all of that danger. The very same guys that I walked past moments earlier decided to attack a man right outside of my apartment. The Lord must have sent angels to watch over me because that was the grace of God. There is a safety when you abide in the presence of the Lord.

"No evil shall befall you, nor shall any plague come near your dwelling; for He shall give his angels charge over you, to keep you in all your ways." (Psalms 91: 10 – 11)

In June 2008 I moved back to London and began living my life with God in the driving seat.

A few months later I joined the drama ministry at my church. I am happy that I still got to do acting, this time all for the glory of God. We have travelled all over the world spreading the gospel message through our divinely inspired plays. God gives people talents and abilities so that He can use them for His glory, not so that we can use them for our glory.

The bible says that: *"Every good gift and every perfect gift is from above and comes down from the Father of lights."* (James 1:17)

It's 2016, 8 years later, I wrote this book and I called it 'Diaries of a Visionary - Inspiring Dreams.' Follow my journey!

CHAPTER 2

'2015' What a Year

Dear Diary,

It's January 2016 and I am reflecting over the past year.

2015 was the year when God began to reveal himself to me on a different level. This is the year that I began to understand what it meant to live by faith. This was a year of testing and trials but God showed me that He is so faithful. God is more than able to fulfil all of His promises. 2015 was the year that I received the gift of prophecy.

Spiritual Gifts!

In 1 Corinthians 14:1 -5, Paul the Apostle said:

"Purse love, and desire spiritual gifts, but especially that you may prophesy. For he who speaks in a tongue does not speak to men but to God, for no one understands him; however in the spirit he speaks mysteries. But he who prophesies speaks edification,

29

exhortation and comfort to men. He who speaks in a tongue edifies himself, but he who prophesies edifies the church. I wish you all spoke with tongues, but even more that you prophesied; for he who prophesies is greater than he who speaks in tongues unless indeed he interprets, that the church may receive edification."

God instructs every believer to 'earnestly desire' spiritual gifts but especially to pursue the gift of prophecy. These day's people earnestly desire everything other than what God has inspired us to earnestly desire. Desire the best gifts!

I first asked for the gift of prophecy in around 2013 or 2014. I initially asked for this gift because I wanted to be closer to God - I wanted to be able to hear God speak and give me clear instructions. I used to be the type of person that would need to gather multiple opinions on a matter before reaching a conclusion. Learning how to discern the voice of God was an amazing transition for me.

The purpose of the gift of prophecy is to encourage the church through edification, exhortation and consolation.

Elevate my Faith!

One day I was in church service and as I was speaking out in tongues during prayer time, a message came to me.

God dropped these Words into my spirit, *"I have ordered your steps, do not be afraid of sudden terror when it comes for I have already gone before you to make a way for you, for I can make a way where there is no way, even in the wilderness because I hold the keys; I open the door that no man can shut and I shut the door that no man can open, just have faith"* says the Lord.

This was something that I had never experienced before, I wasn't sure whether to say the message out so I waited until after the service and shared it with the preacher. He told me that I should've said it. For the next few months I struggled with my nerves as I earnestly prayed and asked God to increase my faith so that I could use this gift.

It's funny how some people try to catch you out at first, they start asking strange questions and acting like you're making up the gift. It really is funny! Don't worry, when God wants to use your life He will baffle the spectators and silence your critics. That's my story. If you've asked God for something then just focus on doing what God has called you to do. God is faithful.

People's reactions were different some positive, some negative but all I know is that the gifts and calling of God are irrevocable (Romans 11:29).

Most people were welcoming and supportive of what God was doing in my life and in our local church. Shortly after I began to prophecy someone from my church showed me Amos 3:7 – *"Surely the Lord God does nothing unless He reveals His secret to His servants the prophets."* This really encouraged me, to know that I could be so close to God that He would tell me secrets.

When our church was going through what some would call a wilderness experience, God told me to say this:

"These things I have allowed that I may test you and know what is in your heart, for you have loved me in the mountains but will you also love me in the valley. For I am taking you on a journey, there will be high's and there will be lows, will you cling to Me in the lows as well as you cling to Me in the highs, for I am taking you somewhere. And I will purge the rebels from among you for you are My body and I must purify you," says the Lord.

God was faithful to fulfil what He told me to say because 2015 was the year when God really purged, purified and set His church in order.

If God calls you to do something for Him, just be obedient, *"Be strong and of good courage"* because God says He is with you wherever you go (Joshua 1:9).

2015 was the year when people really had to learn that God is in control - the Master Orchestrator. Certain plots and schemes had to come to a rapid end in 2015 because unless the Lord builds the house they labour in vain who build it (Psalms 127:1). They really do labour in vain. So we thank God that He always gets the last word:

"I am the Watchman of My House and I am the Gatekeeper of My House, for I stand at the gate and I watch your going in and your coming out therefore commit your way unto Me that your thoughts may be established" says the Lord.

Tucson

In Chapter 1, I wrote about my days of living in New York City with dreams of moving to Los Angeles and living that 'American Dream.' Well 2015 marked 7 years since I had been back to the United States. Seven is the number of completion. I had to apply for a visa to enter the United States. On previous occasions my application had been denied. God knew that if I got that visa a moment earlier I would probably have never come back to London. So in January 2015 I got my US visa, and in June 2015 I went to a bible conference in Tucson Arizona. It was a tremendous week filled with powerful messages and sermons. Afterwards I stopped over in New York with some friends as a pre – birthday celebration. My obsession with America was over and I was able to enjoy New York as a tourist. We went to visit the Statute of Liberty and Ellis Island for the first time. For those that don't know, Ellis Island was the United States busiest immigration station from 1892 until 1954, a very interesting tourist attraction. During my time in New York I missed out on the cultural aspects. We also found some great deals at the New York City shopping outlets.

Faith

2015 was a year when my faith was tested in more ways than one. Trust me I was living on the edge, mountain and valley type living. At the beginning of the year I asked God to help me draw near to Him so that I would be able to go to God before man in every situation. I found myself in situations where no one understood what I was going through but God. It was difficult for me to comprehend at first, I found myself questioning people's intentions and motives, but then I found myself praying more and listening to the voice of God. It was then I began to realise that God was drawing me nearer to Him and revealing His will and purpose to me.

When God tells you a secret or gives you a vision don't get frustrated when it seems like people around you do not understand. The fact of the matter is that it was not for them to understand it was for you to understand.

It took me a while to realise what was going on. It got to the point where I felt like everyone around me was telling me the opposite of what I knew God had already told me. It was around this time that I got a Word of Knowledge from a brother at church:

"Another man is not in control of your life, God is in control of your life because the bible says that the steps of a good man are ordered by the Lord."

This message set me free - I was no longer seeking understanding from other people I rose to a deeper level of faith with God. But now I know what the scripture means in James 4:8, *"Draw near to God and He will draw near to you."* It's an amazing experience to be close to God. Sometimes you feel like you're getting far away from people, but really you're just getting close to God so embrace it. When you're getting close to God you start to see things with a different perspective. You learn to live above life's circumstances. You get to see further than other people, you get to see the things that are unseen. When pigeons are fighting, eagles don't get involved!

If God has already told you something, just focus on that. Don't get involved with the pigeons rise up like the eagle. You have to pick and choose your battles, *"Be still and know that I am God."* (Psalms 46:10)

Those are my life lessons for 2015. I am looking forward to 2016. The year of the Lord's favour; the year of stability, the year of increase; the year of wisdom and the year of salvation.

I also call 2016 the Year of Transformation. Let's see what God does.

CHAPTER 3

My Words are Spirit and They are Life

Dear Diary,

It's 13 January 2016 and I am thinking about the power of words. I have come to realise that words are very, very powerful.

I used to find myself sitting down listening to nonsense. Seriously! Imagine sitting down listening to someone who does not even have a clue what they are talking about. The person has no power to affect or influence God's will for your life – why are you even giving them a platform? David said be careful what you set before your eyes.

"I will set nothing wicked before my eyes." (Psalms 101:3)

I say be careful what you set before your ears.

I will set nothing wicked before my ears!

Opening your mind up to negative words can only have negative effects, words are spirit. Sometimes you can get your hopes up for something that is never going to happen all because you're listening to someone who is telling you what you want to hear. It may sound nice, it may feel good, but it's still a lie. Why give so much time and energy to someone who has absolutely no power to determine or derail the direction of your life? Instead go to God, His Word will never return void.

"So shall My Word be that goes forth from My mouth; It shall not return to Me void, But it shall accomplish that what I please, And it shall prosper in the thing for which I sent it." (Isaiah 55:11)

Don't rack your brain trying to make sense out of nonsense. If someone comes to you with something that does not align with the Word of God for your life then just dismiss and reject those words. It's not your portion.

I used to find myself having mind battles all because I was sitting down over-thinking and over –analysing a situation which stemmed from the meaningless words and opinions of people.

What does God say about your situation? Just listen to that. If people are talking ask yourself, do these words line up with the Word of God for my life? If not then just leave it and fix your eyes on Jesus Christ. God will elevate you, onwards and upwards because He is the King above all Kings.

The Merciful God of Prophecy: *"Anxiety in the heart of man causes depression, but why do you worry, do you not know that My Words are Life? Run to Me! I'm asking you to run to Me and I will hide you underneath My pavilion, for I have called you onto greater things but you must first win the battle in your mind"* says the Lord.

Mind battles are often caused by a conflict of voices in your mind. You must decide who you are going to listen to. Do not listen to the negative words of a man, meditate on it and esteem it as the Word of God. God says that we should meditate on His Word day and night. (Psalms 1:2)

The other day I found myself having a very serious mind battle over a very simple situation. The volume of conflicting information was giving me a headache and I was listening to the wrong voices. Once I stopped listening to the wrong voices I could hear God say, *"My thoughts are not your thoughts My ways are not your ways."* God's ways are higher than ours.

I like this quote: "In order to bring me down you have to be able to reach me."

Mediate on the Word of God and do not lower yourself to a state of confusion by listening to the negative words of a man. People are human! The bible says in James 3:16 that where you have envying and strife come's confusion and every evil work. This means that confusion is evil! When you are in the will of God you have perfect peace, confusion and chaos is not of God. So be careful what you set before your ears.

How do you identify the voice of God? Align it up with his WORD. God has magnified His Word above His own name - Psalms 138:2.

A Practical Approach

I met a young lady whilst searching for a house mate, when she came to view my room she was telling me about her fears and various mind battles that she was having. I showed her my blog post entitled 'My Words are Spirit and they are Life.' I asked her what was causing the anxiety and I told her to write down all of her fears on paper. Then I showed her that these were lies and we must counteract them with the truth. The Word of God is truth.

When we speak the truth over a lie, the truth will always prevail:

- I am afraid of being alone: I will never leave you nor forsake you (Hebrews 13:5);

- I am nothing, I am no one: You are the light of the world (Matthew 5:14);

- No one cares about me, my life is irrelevant: The human spirit is the lamp of the Lord (Proverbs 20:27);

- I will never amount to anything: For I know the thoughts that I think toward you, says the Lord, thoughts of peace and not of evil to give you a future and a hope (Jeremiah 29:11).

There's something about writing the lies down on paper and counteracting them with the Truth that makes a mighty strong battle plan. The young lady said that once she wrote down these truths and began to profess them over her life she started believing in them and she started living them. Shortly afterwards the lady surrendered her life to Jesus Christ and is now on a completely new path.

"It is the Spirit who gives life; the flesh profits nothing. The Words that I speak to you are Spirit and they are life." (John 6:63)

The Merciful God of Prophecy: *"Yield to Me and I will cleanse you from all unrighteousness, only dwell in My house and stay in My Word. For I have esteemed My Word above My name."* says the Lord.

CHAPTER 4

Wisdom is a Free Gift

Dear Diary,

It's 19 January 2016, and strange things are happening all around me. I'm praying for wisdom.

You know when you sit back and watch a situation play out and you're thinking but why did they do this? Why is this person behaving like that? Can they not see? Well maybe they can't. You don't ever want to be that person that people look at and think wow why did they do that? Can they not see?

Wisdom is a Free Gift!

James 1:5 says, *"Let he who lacks wisdom ask and God will give it generously."* God will give it generously.

Recently I have started praying, "Lord give me wisdom and the mind of Christ." Ever since I've started praying this prayer I've started seeing life in a different perspective. I've come to realise, sometimes people say and do things due to a genuine lack of wisdom. Good intentions but no wisdom. It's not enough to just have good intentions; in fact the road to hell is paved with good intentions. We need wisdom.

It's a privilege to be able to see the things that someone else cannot see it means that you are in a position to pray for them. Intercession is the key.

Martin Luther King Jr said it best when he said, "Nothing in all of the world is more dangerous than sincere ignorance and conscientious stupidity."

I used to try and work out situations. Why would they do that? What were they hoping to achieve? It was the sincerity of the ignorance that disturbed me the most. At the end of the day when the blind lead the blind they will both fall into a ditch! Don't be that person, ignorance is dangerous. Wisdom is a free gift.

The reality is that sometimes people just don't know any better – just pray. I've been praying, "Lord give me wisdom and the mind of Christ." I have come to realise that if someone cannot see what they are doing, how are they going to change? It's like getting annoyed at a blind man for walking into a wall. He can't see where he's going and you can't give him back his sight – only God can.

Sometimes people need to get their own experiences - the reason why your testimony is so powerful is because you're talking from your own experience. Sometimes you may watch someone doing something silly, you know exactly how it's going to play out but you can't tell them because they won't understand. They may listen, but they won't understand. If a person cannot see something for themselves then all you can do is pray for them, sit back and relax. God is in control. Wisdom is a free gift!

CHAPTER 5

The Quiet Place

Dear Diary,

It's 28 January 2016, and I can tell that this year is going to be different. The year of the Lord's favour!

Have you ever been in a place where your life seems static? You're applying for jobs everywhere and can't get anywhere? It's so frustrating! God will get your attention.

In Chapter 7 I will write about my journey of financial faith, I call it 'Walking on Water.' But for now I'll just say that I've been working as a contractor for some years now.

There was a period of time when I wasn't getting any work at all. Not even a job as a waitress or handing out leaflets. This is what I call, 'The Quiet Place.' In the quiet place there are no distractions. Sometimes life can get so busy you don't even have time to sit down pray and reflect – Mary Spirit in a Martha world. In case you're wondering Mary sat at the feet of Jesus whilst Martha was always busy. In the quiet place I started asking God what's happening with my life. There was nothing I could do, everywhere I applied I couldn't get anywhere.

Be still and know that I am God!

God got my attention by leading me to a quiet place. The quiet place will change your life. In the quiet place you can hear your own heart – oh the heart. I could hear myself replaying - empty words. It was the sound of unforgiveness. You know when you keep re-telling a story without names? It's a dead story you don't need to keep telling it. Just pray, "God help me to forgive."

It doesn't matter what they said or what they tried to do, forgiveness isn't about them it's always about you.

No Weapon

Remember, God never said that a weapon wouldn't form only that it wouldn't prosper!

Isaiah 54:17, *"No weapon formed against you shall prosper, and every tongue which rises against you in judgment You shall condemn. This is the heritage of the servants of the Lord, and their righteousness is from Me,"* says the Lord.

In the quiet place I realised that I was offended because of a weapon that didn't even prosper.

Lesson of Life: Never linger on why the weapon was formed just be glad that it didn't prosper. Praise Him! Furthermore, Jesus warned us about offences in Matthew 18 - they will come. Jesus said that offences will come.

So really what's the problem? Is it the weapon that didn't even prosper? Or is it an offence that you knew was coming?

The Merciful God of Prophecy: *"Do not be afraid of their threats nor troubled for I am your Keeper, the Lord of Hosts is My name and I watch over you day and night"* says the Lord.

My prayer is Lord help me to be a forgiving person. Lord you forgave me of all my sin's and gave me a new life.

"To forgive is to set a prisoner free and discover that the prisoner was you." (Lewis B Smedes)

Unforgiveness is a spiritual illness, never underestimate it. Live forgiven and let go of the things you cannot control.

CHAPTER 6

Sleepless Nights

Dear Diary,

It's 8 February 2016 and something has been disturbing my sleep.

There are many different reasons why a person may have trouble sleeping. But one thing I know is that God gives His people sleep. It's not God's will for us to be up at night worrying and restless.

Psalms 127:2: *"It is vain for you to rise up early, to sit up late, To eat the bread of sorrows, For so He gives to his beloved sleep."*

I'm up late and I cannot sleep so I'm writing about sleepless nights.

Sometimes anxiety will keep you up all night, but sometimes God will trouble you in your spirit to do something and you won't be able to rest until you do it. Don't take this lightly, make enquiries, not with a counsellor or a doctor - make enquiries with the Lord.

Why can't I sleep Lord? If you're up at night it's time to pray.

God gives His people sleep.

The other night I was just trying to sleep. I was woken up and tormented by a situation that I cannot go into right now. So I started praying. When God lays someone on your heart pray for them!

I said Lord give this person the peace of God that surpasses all understanding. That helped a bit so I carried on praying. You have to make enquiries.

Why can't I sleep? Eventually God showed me that there was something that I had to do and I wasn't going to have rest until I did it. It involved me passing on some information to someone. I tried to get out of this task, I just didn't want to get involved in the situation but I soon came to realise that there is no substitute for obedience. The more I prayed the more that the situation disturbed my peace.

Ultimately, we know that God loves people, so there's probably a greater cause outside of what God is asking you to do. It may not be for your benefit alone but to help someone else in the long run. God may want to teach them something and He's using you to do it. God may be trying to teach you something and you need to be obedient. God desires truth in the inward parts.

There is no substitute for obedience, make enquiries because God requires truth in the inward parts.

When God troubles you in your spirit to do something – just do it. It may be to go and tell this person something! Go and ask this person something! Forgive this person! Forgive yourself! Let this habit go! Whatever it is that God is telling you to do – there is no substitute for obedience.

God gives His people sleep.

Don't worry if you approach the person to tell them some vital truths and they just refuse to accept it. God desires truth in the INWARD parts. So long as you know you have been obedient in doing what God has told you to do then you will have peace.

The Merciful God of Prophecy: *"Do not worry or fret. I am the Lord exercising loving kindness upon all the earth. All of My works are done in righteousness and justice and I desire truth in the inward parts,"* says the Lord.

I have come to realise that every man has to wrestle with his own conscience with God. Do not be fooled, you may go to someone with truth and they act like they don't know what you're talking about - but they do. Leave them to it because God desires truth in the INWARD parts. We are not living to please man we are living to please God.

In my situation, after I passed on the information that was disturbing my sleep I had great peace. I knew that I had done my part and that was all I needed to do.

If someone just wants to live in denial let that be their sleep deprivation and not yours. If someone wants to live in bitterness, let that be their sleep deprivation and not yours. Do your bit.

Great peace comes when you live to please God and not man.

God gives his people sleep.

CHAPTER 7

Faith: Walking on Water

Dear Diary,

It's 20 February 2016 and I've decided to write about my journey of financial faith. I call it walking on water.

Have you ever wondered what it really means to trust God? What is faith?

"Now faith is the substance of things hoped for, the evidence of things not seen." (Hebrews 11:1).

Lawyer Lawyer

"Why do you continue to doubt Me when I have proven myself to you time and time again?" God said.

I was at church, it was 2011. I had graduated from Law School and was in search of my Pupillage, that's the last stage of training to qualify as a Barrister in England. When I graduated from Law School in 2010 I was offered a job as a Paralegal, it was a 2 month contract that turned into a 3 month contract. When the

55

project ended we were let go without notice. That's the nature of the work. But that's how my journey began. At the back of my mind I was only doing these temporary jobs to kill time before getting my Pupillage.

Jehovah Jireh

In the summer of 2010 when I turned 25 I moved out of my dad's house and into my own flat. The freedom and peace was great, but this meant that I had more bills to pay. I was still working as a contractor and still did not have my pupillage.

Around September 2010 it became very quiet in the world of contract paralegals so I didn't work for a bit. In between contracts I would go to the Job Centre and sign on, I would receive housing benefits and a weekly sum of money until my next contract came. Every time I would go to the job centre I would feel a heavy sadness, like I was trapped in an empty cave. Really is this my life? I would wonder. After studying all of these years? God is on my side so how can this really be what it has come to? I would pray for a job and nothing would come for months. It got to the point where I decided to stop signing on and that's when I actually got a job. It happened to me about three times in between contracts – I would go to sign on and then all of a sudden I would get a call or an email to start a new contract. One time I was in a meeting at the Job Centre where they were asking me for my passport but during the meeting I received a phone call inviting me to a telephone interview, I knew that I was going to get the job so I didn't bother to complete the meeting. I did get the job. This was when I began to feel God telling me not to sign on at the job centre even if I am in between contracts I was to learn to lean on God completely. Furthermore, it was only when I went to sign on that God intervened and gave me a job. God was giving me breadcrumbs and letting me know that He was fully in control. God could actually give me a job any time he wanted to. Moving on, so in 2011 I was at church on a Wednesday evening and a sister gave a prophecy:

"Why do you continue to doubt me when I have proven myself to you time and time again?"

I realised that each time I would go to sign on at the Job Centre God would give me a job. So why did I keep going through the motions of signing on? This was a Word for me. God is in control.

After this day I told God that no matter how bad it gets I'm not going back to the Job Centre to sign on. I'm trusting in you Lord. Jehovah Jireh, not Jehovah Giro. I didn't need to gather multiple opinions on this matter I knew that God had spoken to me so clearly.

5 years later

Flash forward, it's 2016 and I still don't have my pupillage! I'm actually in debt BUT I have a roof over my head; food in my fridge; clothes on my back and I'm driving a brand new Peugeot 108. I'm living my best life now. Pray about everything worry about nothing!

"Therefore I say to you, do not worry about your life, what you will eat or what you will drink; nor about your body, what you will put on. Is not life more than food and the body more than clothing?" (Matthew 6:25)

I decided not to worry and I've come too far to turn back now. I saw many miracles along the way, from sums of money all of a sudden appearing in my account, to the Inland Revenue sending me cheques for tax refunds that I didn't even ask for. God is so faithful. It has never been as bad as it is now, this must be a test because I'm in serious debt. But, I'm still living my best life now, I refuse to worry. I prayed for the peace of God that surpasses all understanding; I prayed for direction and guidance in my career and I prayed for favour with my creditors. I pray about everything and I believe that God is in control.

Don't let the devil lie to you. Whenever you are on your purpose the devil will try and distract you and offer you a shortcut. We are not ignorant of his devices.

It is now February 2016 and I am praying for God to direct my steps. I need direction in relation to my career. In January I got a waitressing job at a Hospitality Company but they do not offer regular hours. I've worked for about 20 hours this year, yes I said hours. I haven't worked a normal 9 to 5 job since October 2015. I got a new car in November 2015. I worked at a couple of trade shows and events here and there but right now I don't know where my next pay cheque is coming from and I need the peace of God that surpasses all understanding. God is teaching me what it really means to live by faith. God has a plan.

My Prayer is Lord if I'm having a 'Job' experience please let me keep my car. It's a brand new Peugeot 108 - I love my car. In case you're wondering, when God tested Job He allowed the devil to take away everything that Job owned to see if Job would curse God. Job passed the test.

"Why do you continue to doubt Me when I have proven myself to you time and time again?"

I'm living my best life now because God has designed it that the just shall live by FAITH. *"Now the just shall live by faith; But if anyone draws back, My soul has no pleasure in him,"* (Hebrews 10:38). I refuse to draw back.

What Next...

At the beginning of this quiet season in my life I was earnestly searching for a job every day. Its February 2016. I've actually stopped applying for jobs now, it's time to stop and pray. God is the Maker of heaven and earth. God can do anything, if He really wanted me to work I would have a job right? I know from my past experiences that if God really wanted me to have a job I would have one. There are many things that I can do. There must be a greater purpose for this season of my life. Ok Lord, if you don't want me to work what do you want me to do?

"SIT AT MY FEET AND IN MY PRESENCE YOU WILL BE MADE WHOLE!"

Really Lord you want me to wake up every day and sit at your feet? So that's what I do I literally spend hours praying, reading my bible, listening to music and reading Christian books. I had to let the job search go. This was an opportunity for me to spend time with God. It was actually during this quiet season that I discovered my writing abilities. I have started writing a blog about my life and my experiences. God knows that I have bills to pay He knows all of these things and yet He puts His thumb on me and says:

"Sit at my feet and in My presence you will be made whole."

I've been doing this for the past few weeks and I actually have great peace. I asked for the peace of God that surpasses all understanding. I am not worried about bills I know that God will come through. He is fully in control.

That's how I spend my days, wake up; pray; listen to music; read my bible; read a Christian book and write for my blog. Once in a while I get called in to work for the hospitality company. I've managed to cover all of my bills except for my rent. I recently received a rent arrears letter from the council which I have left on my living room table - Lord you can see that I owe them money I'll leave it in your hands. People have been panicking & sending me job vacancies, but it's alright I know that when God is ready for me I will have a job.

One of my prayers since the beginning of 2016 was for direction and stability in my career. A few days ago I was talking to a friend of a friend at a poetry night. He showed me this, *"I know your works. See I have placed before you an open door, and no one can shut it, for you have a little strength, have kept My word and have not denied mM name."* (Revelations 3:8)

We serve a God who hears and answers prayers! I need to find that open door.

My prayer is, Lord point me towards the open door. Lord show me where my job is and what you want me to do. I'm not trying to get anywhere that God doesn't want me to be. Illuminate my path Lord, show me where you want me to go.

War Room

I started a war room in my living room - those that have seen the film know what I mean - and this is where I have been spending my days with the Lord. I can literally spend hours on end praying, reading and writing.

This Monday someone from church sent me a video of a prophecy that I gave one time during a church service. The person said that they were just deleting videos from their phone and came across it.

God works in mysterious ways because the Word was timely for my current season, God is so faithful.

The Merciful God of Prophecy: *"For I am preparing you for where I am taking you to, though I am grinding you be patient in tribulation and even in the midst of the fiery furnace know that I am with you for I am refining you. And I will bring you out and you will be replenished and then I will launch you forth into a destiny and when you ask Me I will deliver the nations into your hands as your inheritance, for you have been faithful and you have trusted in Me, now is not the time for you to be dismayed now is not the time for you to be anxious but now is the time for you to be steadfast for I am more than able to complete all that I began I am more than able to fulfil all of My promises, do not marvel at what I have said for My Words are Spirit and they are Life,"* says the Lord.

God speaks through me, God speaks to me!

We must walk by faith, because God has designed it that the just shall live by faith. Our best days are ahead and not behind.

CHAPTER 8

She Sits at His Feet because His Presence Makes Her Whole!

Dear Diary,

I have learnt so many things sitting at the feet of Jesus these past few weeks; I will try my best to condense them. God is so good He cares even about the little things! Who am I that you are mindful of me?

These are some of the things that Jesus taught me this week:

- Sit at My feet and in My presence you will be made whole.

- Trust in the Lord with all your heart and lean not on your own understanding, in all of your ways acknowledge Him and he will direct your paths.

- The Lord will perfect that which concerns you.

God is the same yesterday, today and forevermore. Therefore we should trust God wholeheartedly and not try to work Him out. We must learn how to step out of the way so that God can move.

Sit back and relax God is in control

This week God reminded me of the power of His unconditional love. I was sitting on my living room chair talking to Jesus. I was reminded of a time when I was a new convert and I was still running from God as I had bigger plans for my life - so I thought. I wanted to go back to New York, pursue my career in the entertainment industry, no doubt the devil had other plans in store for me. That's the thing with running from God, the devil will show you the bait but not the hook. God is so faithful that He continued to pursue me even when I was going in the wrong direction. He strategically placed people in my life to put me back on course.

"The steps of a good man are ordered by the Lord. And he delights in his way. Though he fall, he shall not be utterly cast down; For the Lord upholds him with His hand." (Psalms 37:23 – 24)

Lord you loved me when I didn't even know what love was. Lord you pursued me.

Conversations with God

This Scripture came to my mind as I was praying this week:

Isaiah 54:5 "For your Maker is your husband, The Lord of hosts is His name; And your Redeemer is the Holy One of Israel; He is called the God of the whole earth."

I felt like this was God's way of letting me know that he was enough for me. I said aloud "Jesus you really are all that I need." That's when God said:

"I'm about to invade your life and turn things around. I want you to remember this present time when it was just Me and you – and you were complete."

Your Maker is your husband! God isn't a God that is confined to the four walls of your house or the four walls of your church. He is the God of the whole earth. Real contentment comes from Christ alone.

"Therefore do not worry, saying, what shall we eat? Or what shall we drink? Or what shall we wear? For after all of these things the Gentiles seek. For your heavenly Father knows that you need all these things. But seek first the kingdom of God and His righteousness, and all these things shall be added to you." (Matthew 6:31 -34)

Contentment comes from Christ alone, everything that is added to you is an additional benefit! Don't get me wrong we all need to have a vision for our lives but my point is that contentment comes from Christ alone.

Vision

The bible says in Proverbs 29:18 that, *"where there is no vision the people perish"* [AMP]. We need a vision that is based on a revelation of God's Word. When you pray God can reveal things to you that already exist in the spiritual realm. Our faith brings these things into the physical realm. Faith is the key that unlocks the door to your destiny.

Hebrews 11:6 says that without faith it is impossible to please God.

We need to see the things that are not there yet, be creative. Don't just look at the here and now, take the boundaries off of your mind you will begin to realise that the best is yet to come. Think about where you want to be in life, pray about it, write about it and speak it into existence. I encourage you to dream big and dream until your dreams come true.

Habakkuk 2:2 says, *"write the vision and make it plain."* So I wrote my vision and I made it plain before

God. What's your vision? Get a journal and start writing down your dreams, your goals and your visions.

Quick Tip: If you tell people your dreams they may try to discourage you, sometimes you just have to keep the vision alive in your own heart.

This week as I was praying a scripture came to my mind. It was Proverbs 15:28, *"The heart of the prudent studies how to answer."* We must remember to pray in advance of situations about how we will respond.

New Boots

This is why I said at the beginning of this diary entry that God cares about the little things! Since the beginning of this year I have wanted to get new black boots. This morning I decided to talk to God about them, I prayed for new boots that were affordable considering my current season of low income and sporadic work shifts. After our church outreach I was walking though the high street and this shop that sales really nice boots were having a 'closing down sale.' So I went inside and I saw these really nice black boots from £40 reduced to £15, they were so nice. I am slightly obsessed with boots, just slightly. Initially the shop didn't have the boots in my size but then all of a sudden they just so happened to find one in my size.

Must be God right? I have to thank God for the little things. He is my Keeper and He watches over me.

God gave us Mothers

On Sunday my mother came to visit me on her way from work, she decided to leave a cheque on my living room table. My mother has been such a great blessing during this season of my life – God's way of reminding me that we are not alone on this earth. God gave us mothers. God has been so faithful and I'm overwhelmed by His continuous blessings. But I know that greater is coming.

"Why do you continue to doubt me when I have proven myself to you time and time again?"

We must always remember to let God be true and every situation a lie!

Matthew 6:31 -33 says, *"Therefore do not worry, saying 'What shall we eat? Or 'What shall we drink?' or 'What shall we wear?' For after all these things the Gentiles seek, For your heavenly Father knows that you need all these things. But seek first the kingdom of God and His righteousness, and all these things SHALL be added to you."*

Psalms 37:25 says, *"I have been young and now I am old, yet I have never seen the righteous forsaken or his descendants begging bread."*

These are God's promises not the words of a man! God has been faithful to keep his promises towards me.

CHAPTER 9

Polishing Glasses

Dear Diary,

It's March 2016, a few months into the year and I think I'm starting to understand this season a bit better.

In January I got a job working for a hospitality and events company. I believe that this job was divinely orchestrated. God sent me there. I was just applying for random jobs and getting no response, but this particular company emailed me back straight away and invited me in for an induction day. The weird thing about this company is that they don't give you set days and hours to work, you email them on a weekly basis and let them know when you are available. So it was like I had a job but not really. I still had to live by faith because every week I would send them an email with my availability not knowing whether they would give me any shifts for the following weeks. There were still weeks where I would email them and they wouldn't have any work.

God has a sense of humour. The first shift that I was given was on a Thursday evening and I was told to wear a black shirt and trousers. I went out and brought a black shirt and trousers, only to be told a couple of hours beforehand that my shift had been cancelled. The following day I was emailed with a replacement shift for the following week but this time I had to go out and buy a white shirt. I haven't been working for the past 3 months and they give me one shift for four hours. First I have to go out and buy a black shirt then I have to go out and buy a white shirt. God really does have a sense of humour. I refuse to complain knowing that God is in control.

Sometimes God will send you to places in order to teach you things and build your character. I believe that God sent me to this hospitality company to improve my time-keeping and also to develop within me a character of humility. Most of the staff working for this company are from foreign countries and don't really have much choice in relation to jobs. The way that they are treated can sometimes be ridiculous. There was one particular shift where I worked for 15 hours at the Intercontinental Hotel in Greenwich. I had to start work at 7.30am and I didn't finish work until 11pm.

"Do not despise the chastening of the Lord, nor detest His correction; For whom the Lord loves He corrects."
(Proverbs 3:11)

Polishing Glasses

There were some good days after that. The next time I went back to the Intercontinental Hotel, I was standing there 'polishing glasses' with another waiter from Bulgaria. He said that he had travelled to London in order to undertake his Master's Degree at Coventry University. The same way I used to think America was so special, it was almost like he felt the same way about England.

"What do you think about Coventry University?" He asked me.

I told him that I didn't know anything about Coventry as I went to Kings College London.

"You have a degree in London!" He exclaimed.

I said, "Yes I studied Law at Kings."

"Really, so what are you doing here?" He asked.

"I'm working just like you are – I'm polishing glasses." I replied.

The waiter explained that it doesn't make sense to him, "This is like the lowest of the low, you do not need any qualifications to do this job." When you are walking by faith, sometimes things just don't make sense.

The bible says that, *"The message of the cross is foolishness to those who are perishing."* (1 Corinthians 1:18)

This guy is thinking that once he gets to Coventry University and completes his Master's Degree then he will have a great job and life will be complete. It doesn't make sense to him that I already have a law degree from a top London University and I am standing here with him polishing glasses.

I started telling him my story. I said that I am actually on a journey with God at the moment, I explained to him that I have been praying for direction in relation to my career and this is the pathway through which God has taken me. He said he doesn't believe in God, he said he's an Atheist. I told him that it takes faith to believe in God. Take my life as an example. I already have the things that you are searching for but I believe that God sent me here for a season and for a purpose, that's why I am here. It doesn't make sense to you because I'm living by faith – faith is the substance of things hoped for, the evidence of things not seen. I'm taking my instructions from an invisible God. I know that God wants the best for me and I trust Him to get me there. This is what it means to walk by faith. I told the waiter, it may sound strange but it takes faith to believe in God.

"For the message of the cross is foolishness to those who are perishing, but to us who are being saved it is the power of God." (1 Corinthians 1:18)

The Message of the Cross

What is the message of the cross? That the Almighty God himself stepped down from heaven in the form of a Man in order to seek and save lost souls by dying on a cross for our sins. Jesus was an innocent Man and He died so that we could be free. It takes faith to obtain the promises of God.

After we finished our conversation we went our separate ways. A few moments later I was walking through the corridor humming a gospel song under my breath. The Bulgarian waiter who told me he was an Atheist, walked by.

"So do you go to church every Sunday? He asked.

"Yes I go to church on Sundays and Wednesday as well." I replied and continued walking.

God had used me to ignite something inside of him that day because now he is asking questions about God. Completeness cannot be found in a Master's degree, real contentment comes from Jesus Christ. Just as I went to America in search of purpose, he was doing the same thing in London. I was able to pass on the revelation that "good things come from above and not from abroad."

All of this happened whilst I was standing there polishing glasses. Polishing Glasses!

This really encouraged me to trust God even when things don't seem to be going the way that we expect. I'm praying for direction and stability in my career and I end up with a waitressing job. God was able to use me in that place. Sometimes God has to take you back to the basics so that you can have a firm foundation later on in life.

"For as the heavens are higher than the earth, so are My ways higher than your ways, And My thoughts than your thoughts." (Isaiah 55:9)

CHAPTER 10

What's My Purpose?

Dear Diary,

Have you ever asked this question? What is the purpose of my life?

Ok, so this was another one of my prayers at the start of the year - Lord reveal to me my purpose! I was looking for something specific - God what did you create me to do? Imagine how sad it would be to get to the end of your days and not even fulfil your purpose on the earth! There are some prayers that God will answer almost immediately; others can take months or even years for God to answer! One thing I know is that God has a purpose for everything that He created.

"To everything there is a season, A time for every purpose under heaven." (Ecclesiastes 3:1)

Lord what's my Purpose?

"I created you for you to worship Me." What does this mean though? *"I created you for My glory."* (Isaiah

43:7) When God looks at your life do you make Him look good?

The sermon at church last Sunday was on worship and it answered all of my questions on purpose. I need to go deeper. God is so faithful. Your life needs to bring God glory, everywhere you go, in everything you do – God says *"I created you for you to worship Me."* The devil desires to be worshiped but only Jesus deserves to be worshiped! Everything about you was handcrafted by God. We have to know that we owe Him everything!

Eve's Purpose

When Eve was in the Garden of Eden, she lost sight of her purpose! God created her from the rib of Adam he called her to be a wife and a helper to Adam, but first and foremost Eve was created in the image of God. For His Glory!

Genesis 1:27 says"...*in the image of God He created him; male and female He created them.*"

Eve was one of God's image bearers on the earth. But she forgot her purpose. In Genesis Chapter 3 Eve was in the Garden of Eden and she started confiding in the serpent (the devil) talking about how God told them not to eat of the tree in the midst of the garden. But the thing is - Why was Eve talking to the devil? She was created in the image of God. For His glory! Why was she sharing God's secrets with the devil? See Eve forgot her purpose!

I Created you for you to worship Me!

In Genesis 3:6 we read that Eve ate of the forbidden fruit and then gave some to Adam to eat as well, she didn't forget that she was a wife, she remembered to feed her husband! But she didn't remember that she was created by God For His glory! When God asked her what happened she said "the serpent deceived me and I ate." The serpent deceived her because she gave him a platform to speak. As a result God had to banish them from the Garden. See Eve was talking to the devil instead of listening to God, when you do that you lose sight of the reason why you were created.

"I created you for you to worship Me! For My Glory!"

Whilst praying about this topic I was reminded of the words that my Pastor spoke to me before I left New York in 2008 to move back to London. He said, "I believe that you're saved but you still want to be in the driving seat of your life, when you get saved you have to let God be in the driving seat." He told me to go home and pray about where God wants me to be – so I did – and God told me quite quickly that I was supposed to go back to London - so I did. Pastor Robert also said that I have a characteristic that draws people. He said, "God gave you that so He could use it for His glory, not so that you could use it for your glory!"

So there we have it – "I created you for My glory".

When I initially asked this question I wanted something specific, like what exactly do I do Lord, how do I bring You glory Lord? God told me not to lose myself. He said think about your greater purpose on this earth and think about how you can be a blessing to someone, whatever season of life you are in. Some people just spend their whole single life waiting for marriage, it's a waste of a whole season of life. Use your singlehood to bless someone. When you are pursuing your purpose God will meet all of your needs.

A Practical Approach

We need to take practical steps in finding out God's purpose for our lives. How exactly do we bring Glory to God in our individual lives?

I am reminded of the parable of the talents in Matthew 25. The reality is that God has given each person different gifts and talents, you may have the gift of speaking, you may be able to speak words that change people's lives - use it for His glory. You may have the talent to sing, then sing people out of bondage; out of death; hell and the grave - use it for His glory. You may have a good memory, you can memorise scripture and it rolls off of your tongue - use it for His glory. If your talent is writing then write for God. When you are pursuing your purpose you will discover talents you didn't even know that you had.

I created you for you to worship Me!

"Every good and perfect gift is from above and comes down from the Father of lights." (James 1:7)

God gave us these things so that He could use them and not so that we could misuse them!

My prayer is, Lord you have given me all of these talents and abilities; show me what you want me to do! Lord illuminate my path and teach me how to walk in my purpose!

See now is not the time to be seeking counsel from the devil! Don't be like Eve, making moves with the serpent when you should be talking to God!

Find your passion, pursue Christ and live out your purpose. God doesn't make any mistakes! Everything that He created has a purpose!

For His glory! I created You for You to Worship Me.

CHAPTER 11

The Open Door

Dear Diary,

Towards the end of last year, I went to visit my father. He reminded me that I have tried this law career for almost for 5 years now, I have gotten so close to getting my pupillage but still no joy. He said I should go back to school, maybe study medicine instead. Ok so that was never going to happen, I knew that medicine was not for me. I also dismissed anything to do with banking and finance. It's not for everyone! But I did acknowledge that it was time for me to let go and let God show me what to do next. All I had ever studied from the age of 18 was law. Law degree from London, New York Bar and the Bar of England and Wales! It's all I knew really. Maybe this was just something else that I was holding on to from my old life? I wanted to be an Entertainment Lawyer when I lived in America then I changed it to Barrister when I moved back to London. Maybe God wants me to do something else, at least for now anyway.

Giving you my DREAMS

Towards the end of 2015 I remember lifting my hands to God and saying, "I'm giving you my dreams." I meant it with all of my heart. I didn't want to get anywhere that God didn't want me to be. Whether it was an actress or a lawyer whatever the case, God I'm giving you my dreams.

My dad gave me three guidelines to follow when looking for a new career. He said that I should write them down. So I did. Write your vision and make it plain:

- Percentage of people that get jobs after they graduate

- How good is the remuneration in this career

- How long can I work in this profession before I retire

I used these guidelines, and I said God illuminate my path and show me what to do next.

I went to visit a friend of mine and we ended up brainstorming and creating a spider diagram of my different hobbies and talents. She asked me what I am good at and I said writing, acting and talking. What do I see myself doing? I said I see myself speaking on a subject. What is my favourite hobby, I said reading. Although I loved English Literature at school I wasn't much of a reader until I entered into this quiet season of life and took a break from my job as a Paralegal. I discovered a passion for reading books and writing short stories. The sense of release that I experienced after writing my first blog was amazing. I have been writing ever since. My passion for literature has been reignited.

Back to the point, so my friend and I prayed that God would give me boldness in finding a job. I kept the spider diagrams that we had created, I went home and I continued praying. I said, "God point me towards that open door."

Once I put all of these factors together, including the advice that my dad gave me, a sense of divine inspiration came over me. What do I enjoy? What am I good at? What do I see myself doing? Well, I see myself reading, writing and speaking on a subject. Maybe I can be an English teacher!

I sat down in my room and started to envision myself as an English teacher. I didn't actually think about that before this day, it was like a revelation. Have I discovered my true calling? Follow my journey.

CHAPTER 12

The Waiting Game

Dear Diary,

Ok so does this happen to you or is it just me? The question on everyone's lips soooo when are you getting married? People are funny I don't really know what they want me to say. Don't worry about what I'm doing worry about why you're worried about what I'm doing. My future is in God's hands! God knows. When you become accustomed to living your life for Christ there are certain things that become essential – one of them is trusting God. When they keep talking!

The real question they should be asking is – teach me how to wait! Marriage is not the end of the game, even after you get married, you still have to wait on God! Don't get distracted by what God is doing in someone else's life – just wait. People always want to question what God is doing.

"Where were you when I laid the earth's foundation?" (Job 38:4)

Waiting is Trusting

Well, these days people put their trust in all kinds of things, when you go on holiday you buy a ticket and board a plane, you trust the pilot to get you to your destination right? You don't keep running up to the front of the plane asking him questions – are we still going to America? Not China? Are you sure you're going in the right direction? Can I see your pilot's license please? You don't sit down panicking the whole journey worrying about whether you will make it to your destination? You don't take matters into your own hand and start trying to fly the plane yourself! You sleep; you watch films; you chat to friends; you WAIT and believe that the pilot will get you to your destination. Right? Well that's what it means to trust. Jesus is the pilot, waiting is trusting.

When they keep asking you why you're not married!

One night I was talking on the phone to my friend about this whole subject of marriage & I fell asleep with my bible next to my pillow. When I opened my bible in the morning, it opened straight onto the page of the story of Isaac and Rebekah in Genesis 24. For those that don't know the story - Rebekah went to draw water from the well of water, she met some strangers at the well and decided to bless them, she gave them water to drink and also drew water for their camels. Little did Rebekah know that these strangers were servants coming to find a bride for Isaac they were looking for the woman that would say 'Drink, and I will also give your camels a drink'. Although Rebekah was very beautiful to behold (Genesis 24:16) she didn't go and entice anyone. Rebekah was a servant's answered prayer! It's he who finds, not she who finds. Proverbs 18:22, *"He who finds a wife finds a good thing and obtains favour from the Lord."*

A Servant's Answered Prayer

A sister once told me that trying to be a matchmaker is like trying to play God and it's so true. If you have to force it just leave it alone, friendships, relationships, ponytails just leave it! Let God write your story. God is the Master Orchestrator! I have been saved for over 8 years now and I have witnessed many spiritual tragedies, strong women of God being taken out of the script that God has for them all in the name of wanting to be married! Taking matters into their own hands. Jesus I wouldn't trade you for the world!

So I've decided to write a message about waiting on God.

Why wait on God?

Well, God already knows everything. The future belongs to those who see it beforehand! God knows the end from the very beginning.

God has a plan for your life, do not allow fear and desperation to take you out of the script. God can even tell you when you're getting married, He can tell you who you are going to marry – but can God trust you? God does not contradict Himself.

Proverbs 18:22 says, *"He who finds a wife finds a good thing and obtains favour from the Lord."*

He who finds! God is the one that woke Adam up and showed him who his wife was – and so shall it be for you if only you will just wait and trust God. God has secrets but the question is can God trust you?

It is a characteristic of wisdom not to do desperate things. Like I said in Chapter 4, wisdom is a free gift!

I was having a discussion with a sister from church the other day, she was talking about some of the reasons why people find it hard to wait on God. I've addressed a couple of the reasons below.

Love or Lust?

Well the thing is, the flesh is never satisfied – it has been preached on time and time again, getting married does not solve your lust problem only Jesus can! If that's the reason why you're rushing then you need to sit down and pray. If marriage could solve a lust problem then there would be no such thing as divorce! Galatians 5:16 says, *"...walk in the spirit and you shall not fulfil the lust of the flesh."* Some people are just being led by the flesh and using the word 'marriage' to make it sound spiritual! This is warfare.

Galatians 5:17 says, *"For the flesh lusts against the Spirit and the Spirit against the flesh; and these are contrary to one another..."* You must crucify the flesh.

Ephesians 4:22 - 23 instructs, *"That you PUT OFF, concerning your former conduct the old man which grows corrupt according to the deceitful lusts and be renewed in the spirit of your mind."*

It's time to pray: Spirit crucify my flesh so that I can live for God! Jesus teach me how to live!

Lonely?

The single life is not the lonely life – loneliness is being married to someone that doesn't love you. Don't rush it and don't force it – your Maker is your husband. God says He will, *"Never leave you nor forsake you."* (Hebrews 13:5) Get to know Jesus because true contentment can only be found in Jesus Christ. If you are waiting for a man, a mere human being, to come and fill a void of loneliness then you will be disappointed! Only Jesus can fill that void. Jesus is the source of life!

So Why Wait?

The future belongs to those who see it beforehand. Wait on God's best!

Do not compare yourself to others because everyone's journey is unique. There are people that got saved around the same time as me, some are married, some have backslid, some tried to force it! You should never let someone else's journey distract you from your destination.

As you wait on God the devil will try and distract you & offer you a short cut.

My Prayer is Spirit of TRUTH keep me undeceived.

There are many references in the bible where Gods says those that wait on the LORD shall not be put to shame!

- Isaiah 49:23, "Then you will know that I am the Lord, For they shall not be ashamed who wait for Me."

- Psalms 25:3, "Indeed, let no one who waits on You be ashamed."

- Romans 10:11, "For the Scripture says, Whoever believes on Him will not be put to shame."

These are God's promises not the words of a man. Fix your eyes on Jesus! Waiting is trusting so fix your eyes on Jesus and wait on God's best.

CHAPTER 13

Who Am I?

Dear Diary,

I used to struggle with my identity, knowing who I am. Do you ever experience a fear of rejection wanting so badly to be accepted by people? This was me once upon a time, but Jesus showed me the power of His unconditional love and that I am accepted by Him.

Psalms 139:14, *"I will praise you because I am FEARFULLY and WONDERFULLY made."*

Now let us drop the man-pleasing spirit. I'm writing about the man-pleasing spirit because I believe that it stems from a fear of rejection. Don't let anybody put a label on you because Christ has put a value on you!

When we bowed our knee for salvation God saved us from our sins not from ourselves. What does that mean? Well as believers we are being transformed daily into the image of Christ (2 Corinthians 3:18) not into the image of any other human being! Do not allow another human being to dictate or define who you should be in Christ. God says "I made you." People want to define you so that they can confine you – that's how you miss your destiny! Where God is taking you is a personal journey, allow Him to mould you. God is the author of my destiny. The Lord sees not as man sees, *"Man looks at the outward appearance but the LORD looks at the heart."* (1 Sam 16:7)

About 6 years ago I received a prophetic word from a brother at my church:

"People try to label you and put you in a box. God says don't listen to what they say about you listen to what I say about you" What do you say Lord? "I say just focus on Me and I'm going to raise you up."

People are too busy looking to the left and right, look up because God wants to raise you up.

At the end of the day God is the one that raises people up! (Ephesians 4:11) God is the one that distributes spiritual gifts. (1 Corinthians 12:11)

We are being transformed daily into the image of Christ. (2 Corinthians 3:18)

There's no need trying to conform to the image of another man because Jesus himself said that He had no need that anyone should testify of man for He knew all men (John 2:24 – 25). So let us drop the man –pleasing spirit!

God Made You to Be You

I've come to realise, people will always have their opinion's, I can't allow anyone to put me in a box and let that get in the way of me fulfilling my destiny in Christ.

My prayer - Lord I come against the spirit of offence. It's a spirit. Jesus had to warn us about the spirit of offence in Matthew 18.

Who are you?

OK so how do you see yourself, examine yourself. How do people describe you? Do you bear witness to that? People say that I'm spiritual, a good listener, outspoken.

A wise man once told me –"If people have a problem with the way that you are, that is not your problem that is their problem."

She speaks like God is speaking through her!

Galatians 5:22 talks about the fruit of the Holy Spirit, these are love, joy, peace, longsuffering, kindness, goodness, faithfulness, gentleness and self-control. These are the things to strive for, but as for your own personality traits, your quirks and your sense of humour: that's your business, be yourself. Let us drop the man –pleasing spirit!

Someone once advised me not to be sarcastic. Don't be sarcastic!

Well Elijah was a mighty prophet of God. In 1 Kings 18: 27 he was being sarcastic when he was mocking the prophets of Baal. Why did God put that in the bible? Everyone has their own gifts, talents and characteristics. Never let another man dictate who you should be in Christ!

Recently I have been really praying for God to show me Who I am! How do you see me Lord? I asked God to set me free from caring too much about what people say because Ecclesiastes 7:1 says do not take everything that people say to heart. When you care too much, it's too much.

The Merciful God of Prophecy: *"I made you! In My own image I made you and you are fearfully and wonderfully made. I am the Lord and I make no mistake. For I am the Potter and you are My clay and I have moulded you. And I am He that chips away at your transgressions so far as the east is from the west I have removed your transgressions from you and I have blotted out your sins and your lawless deeds for My* *own sake. For you are Mine and you belong to Me. And I have accepted you,"* says the Lord.

Thank you for keeping me all of these years Lord!

Do not let anyone put a label on you because Christ has put a value on you. I don't look to any man to validate my worth and tell me who I am – I look to Jesus . Who am I? "You are mine and I HAVE ACCEPTED YOU," says the LORD.

At the end of the day if you cannot come to me with something constructive and backed – up by the Word of God then: What spirit are you of? If it's not a sin and it's not a transgression then it's just an opinion. God called us to love people not to try and change them. This is why we must drop the man-pleasing spirit! Remember who you're living for.

Even when man rejects you God says I HAVE ACCEPTED YOU!!!!!

Live to please God and not man, know who you are.

CHAPTER 14

Do You See What I See?
Be A Visionary

Dear Diary,

The other day I saw a photograph of a pigeon looking at its reflection in the water, but when this pigeon looked at his reflection he saw not a pigeon, he saw a bald eagle. This pigeon had dreams, in his mind he saw himself as an eagle. This pigeon wasn't fighting with the rest of the pigeons because he was too busy looking at the eagle. This was not just an ordinary pigeon, he was a visionary. There's a reason why the pigeons are fighting over breadcrumbs and the eagle isn't. The eagle is high and lifted up. It can see the bakery in the distance. In fact, the eagle knows the baker. Jesus is the Baker.

Jesus calls himself the bread of life.

John 6:35, *"I am the bread of life. He who comes to Me shall never hunger, and he who believes in Me shall never thirst."*

The eagle doesn't need to be fighting over breadcrumbs and scavenging around on the ground because he knows the One who makes all of the bread. The pigeon only sees what's here and now but the eagle can see in the distance and he knows that the best is yet to come.

The Pigeon and the Eagle: Do you see what I see?

Pigeons are actually highly intelligent animals, one of only 6 species, and the only non-mammal to have the ability to recognise its own 'mirror' reflection. They are incredibly complex and highly intelligent animals. However, when the pigeon in the photograph that I saw looks at his reflection he sees not a pigeon but he sees a bald eagle. The pigeon is a creative visionary, he sees the things that are not there yet. We need to see the things that are not there yet.

Hebrews 11:1 says, *"Now faith is the substance of things hoped for, the evidence of things not seen."*

It takes faith to obtain the promises of God.

Eagles have vision, even when an eagle sits still its head will be tilted side to side to observe what is happening all around it. Eagles eyes are specifically designed for long distance focus and clarity. Sometimes you have to look at things not just for what they are but for what they can become!!!

The future belongs to those who see it beforehand

When you look at yourself what do you see? Do you see what you are or what you can become? Do you see what I see? The photograph got me thinking about the attributes of a pigeon and the attributes of an eagle.

Pigeons are found in low places, they will go wherever they see food. On the other hand, eagles are found in high places, they can fly up to the altitude of 10,000 feet. At 10,000 feet you will never find another bird!

Isaiah 40:31 says, *"But those who hope in the LORD will renew their strength. They will soar on wings like eagles; they will run and not grow weary, they will walk and not be faint."*

There are no references to pigeons in the bible! This means that you and I were made for high places!

CHAPTER 15

The Brokenhearted

Dear Diary,

I dedicate this chapter to my dear little brother Jefe Okobia born 13.04.95 – 29.06.04.

Dear brother, it's the 13th April 2016, and you would have been 21 years old today. We know that God heals the brokenhearted because Psalms 147:3 says, *"He heals the brokenhearted And binds up their wounds."*

Dear Brother

You lived a short but meaningful life, you will be dearly missed. 9 years we had to spend with you. God's precious child! Dear brother. You were such a good boy, so quiet, so kind. When I thought of you today tears flooded my eyes but I heard your little voice saying "Don't cry Des," then I looked up and smiled as I remembered where you are now. I know that you are safe and that you are with Jesus because you believed in Him. Even at the tender age of 8 during the last days of your life you were asking to do your Holy Communion. You made sure you did that Holy Communion! This to me is a symbol of how much you knew and loved Jesus Christ and for that reason I know that you are safe. God's precious child! Dear Brother.

I spoke Psalms 147:3 back to myself today - He heals the brokenhearted and binds up their wounds.

1 Thessalonians 4: 13 – 18: talks about believers who have died. In short, the Scripture says that as Jesus died and rose again, we believe that on His return God will bring with Jesus those who have fallen asleep in him. The dead in Christ shall rise first, after that the believers who are still alive will be caught up together with him. And so we will be with the Lord forever.

Do Not Cry For Me

Do not cry for me Dear Sister. Do not be ignorant.

Those who fall asleep in Christ will rise again.

This means I am not dead but I am alive with Him.

Do not cry for me for I am not gone.

My flesh may have died but my spirit lives on.

Until we meet again. Dear Sister.

Poem by Miss Dee Ok

I just want to encourage anyone that has ever lost a loved one, speak the Word of God back to yourself. Be still and know that God is close to the brokenhearted.

The Merciful God of Prophecy: *"Be still and know that I am close to the brokenhearted, I will bind up all your wounds. Cleave to Me and I will pull you out of the troubled waters, even out of the deepest waters for I was with you in the wilderness throughout all of your wanderings I was there I am reaching out to you cleave to Me and I will uphold you with my righteous right hand and you will be My people and I will be Your God, And you will seek Me, and you will find Me when you search for Me with all of your heart. For I am the Lord who pulled you out of the darkness and into My marvellous light and I set your feet upon a rock and I have established a plan for you. Though thousands may fall at your left hand and at your right hand and though an army may encamp against you, do not fall back. Only stand! Pick up your sword and your shield and put on the full armour, for I have given you the power to trample over witches and serpents and demons and all of the powers of the enemy. For you are My chosen people. And as it was in the days of Abraham and as it was in the days of Noah, so shall it be in your days. If only you will just stand and have faith in these perilous times, in these last days. Do not fall back, but pick up your sword and follow after Me. Bare all things, endure* *all things and know that I am with you even until the end of the ages,"* says the Lord.

CHAPTER 16

The Wilderness Let God Make You

Dear Diary,

Today my house mate gave me a cactus plant. As I was thinking and talking to my house mate about the cactus I became inspired to write this story.

Sometimes when we are going through hard and tough times, our first instinct is to run away! Run away from our problems, run away from tests and trials, run away from difficulties. But there comes a time when you just have to stand firm and let God make you. God made the cactus! Will you let God make a cactus out of you? God wants us to be strong so that we can survive in all types of conditions and circumstances.

In Philippians 4:12, Paul said:

"I know how to be abased, and I know how to abound. Everywhere and in all things I have learned both to be

full and to be hungry, both to abound and to suffer need."

Paul was like the cactus, he was able to survive in all types of circumstances, rich or poor, hot or cold, with plenty and with little. God made the cactus to be a survivor.

I'm talking about the cactus because God made the cactus. But will you let God make you?

The cactus is a member of the plant family, it is not bright and colourful like most plants, but the cactus has great substance. The cactus can survive in all types of weathers and conditions whether as a houseplant or even in the dessert. Since cacti live in dry areas they are able to absorb large amounts of water and store it in the stem or root for periods of drought. Like us, cacti can have dormant periods and periods of intense growth and blossoming. The cactus can survive in the wilderness, in extremely dry conditions where all other plants would have withered away and died – the cactus still survives. God wants us to be like the cactus, able to survive in all types of circumstances and situations!!!

The Wilderness

These past few years I have been having a wilderness experience, tests and trials and all sorts of things, but

God has been making me. There have been times where God has given me just enough to survive. I felt like the Prophet Elijah in 1 Kings 17 when God sent him to camp beside the Brook Cherith. God gave Elijah just enough to survive. God used various methods to provide for Elijah, first He sent the ravens to feed him, then he used a widow at Zarephath. Elijah was in the wilderness, but he was obedient, he did all that the Lord commanded him. God always provides for His people. Will you let God make you?

There were a couple of times this week where I received a morning call from my events staffing agency. I went in; worked for a few hours; ate lunch and was sent home early as they were not as busy as expected. It has been quite funny, it's almost like God just sent me to these places to eat and do some work for Him.

I met a lady whilst serving at a dinner party, she just so happened to be an ex-attendee of my church in Birmingham. We ended up talking during our short break and I was able to invite her to the London branch. Call it a coincidence but I believe in divine appointments.

During this season of my life, I decided not to complain to God about why I have to do these waitressing jobs, instead I decided to let God make me. I have learnt so many things especially over these past few months.

I have come to realise, even if you are not happy with your current season, remember it is just a season and everything happens for a reason. When you are going through a wilderness experience just stay in your place and be obedient because God has not forgotten you!

In Jeremiah 15:20 God told the prophet Jeremiah:

"And I will make you to this people a fortified bronze wall; And they will fight against you, but they shall not prevail against you For I am with you to save you. And deliver you."

This meant that in the day of Jeremiah's ministry he would have all kind of forces fighting against him, saved or unsaved but they were not going to prevail. This scripture came to my mind the other day whilst I was playing netball. I felt God telling me the same thing He told Jeremiah – I will make you to this people a fortified bronze wall, they shall fight against you but they shall not prevail. See when you are going through difficulties or you are going through a wilderness experience you just have to let God make you. In the end it will all be worth it because you will be FORTFIED - all those who are fighting against you will not prevail, they will become frustrated and you will be the one standing and smiling.

Jeremiah 20:11 *"But the Lord is with me as a mighty awesome One. Therefore my persecutors will stumble, and will not prevail. They will be greatly ashamed, for they will not prosper. Their everlasting confusion will never be forgotten."*

Psalms 37:12 – 13 *"The wicked plots against the just, and gnashes at him with his teeth. The Lord laughs at him For he sees that his day is coming."*

Let God make you, God made the cactus!

Have you ever tried to attack a cactus plant? The cactus has a prickly skin to ward off its predators. Anyone silly enough to try and attack a cactus plant will end up getting hurt and the cactus will be standing strong. Look at the stance of a cactus, middle part firmly rooted in the ground, left and right arms out in a flexed muscle position. The stance of the cactus is saying "I shall not be moved".

God made the cactus, will you let God make you?

CHAPTER 17

Divine Appointments

Dear Diary,

2016 has been a great year so far, one of the highlights of my year was attending a prophetic conference in March. It was amazing, a divine appointment.

One of my motto's for this year has been 'pray about everything worry about nothing.' One thing that I have begun to do differently this year is to actually write down my prayer requests before God. Sometimes I write my prayer requests on post it notes and stick them on my bedroom cabinet.

Last month I received a personal invite to an event that was being hosted by a Christian Radio station; I don't really know how they got my details to be honest because I don't actually listen to their station. Initially I wasn't going to attend. It just so happened that a friend of mine got invited to the same event under the same circumstances. We decided to go and check it out.

We met a couple of ladies at the Christian Radio event; one of them said that she was hosting a conference in a couple of weeks which would feature prophets from all over the world. There were going to be presentations, personal prophecies and different workshops. It sounded quite interesting. Will they tell me the same things about my life that God has already told me? I have never been to anything like this before but we decided to go and have a look. I believe in divine appointments.

The first evening that we attended, my friend received a personal prophecy, the second evening we attended I received a personal prophecy. We were told to pray about anything that we heard – the bible says, *"...do not believe every spirit, but test the spirits, whether they are of God."* (1 John 4:1).

I received some very accurate prophecies and confirmations about things to come. The reason I say that the prophecies were accurate is because the prophet was confirming things that God had already spoken to me, there were other things that I could bear witness to as well. He called the next season of my life the season of acceleration. Test the spirits!

Back to School

One of the things that the prophet said to me was this:

"I don't know if you have finished school but I see you back in school doing some things, finishing some things that you started..."

As I mentioned, since the beginning of the year I have been praying for direction in my career. I recently sent off an application and got invited to attend an assessment day at a company called 'Teach First'. I took the prophetic word as confirmation, God wants me to go back to school and be a teacher.

My faith was tested when I received an email following the assessment centre and stating that I did not get on to the 'Teach First' programme. I knew that I had heard from God. There must be some sort of mistake, so I thought. I was almost convinced that I was going to get onto the programme. I didn't understand, and I couldn't call them because it was the bank holiday weekend. I just had to wait.

"I don't understand." I kept saying.

"Trust in the Lord with all your heart, and lean not on your own understanding; In all your ways acknowledge Him and He shall direct your paths."(Proverbs 3:5-6)

I decided to stop trying to understand things and stop trying to work things out. God said go back to school but He didn't specify how I was going to get there. I held on to the prophetic Word that I received and continued to trust God.

Later on that week I began exploring different routes into teaching. I ended up applying for a different programme called 'Schools Direct' which is similar to 'Teach First' but with a different ethos. Teach First is a charity that specialises in placing graduates into challenging schools and training them to be leaders. Schools Direct places graduates into schools and trains them to be outstanding teachers.

A few days after sending off my Schools Direct Application I received a phone call from one of my chosen providers. The lady was interested to know my story of why I was changing from law into teaching. So I told her. About a week later I was invited to attend an assessment day at the schools head office. One of the applicants that I met at the assessment day said that she found the assessment day quite intense. I didn't find it intense at all, partly due to my previous experience at the Teach First assessment. Everything happens for a reason! The Teach First assessment lasted for a full day whereas the Schools Direct assessment lasted for just a few hours. I realised that my previous experience had prepared me for what was to come. It was all part of the process. Lean not on your own understanding! Furthermore I was able to use the skills and experience that I gained in my waitressing job to fill out my application form for the teaching job. When you walk with God nothing that you go through will be in vain.

"And we know that all things work together for good to those who love God, to those who are the called according to His purpose." (Romans 8:28)

A couple of hours after the assessment I received a phone call informing me that I was successful and that they would like to set up an interview with the Principal of the school that I would potentially be working at. I attended the interview with the Principal, Vice Principal, Head of Faculty and Head of the English Department on the Friday of that same week. Later on that day I was offered a position at the school as a trainee English teacher starting in September. This all happened really quickly - finally after these years of searching for a stable career, the day has come. God always comes through. 2016 the year of stability, the year of increase, the year of the Lord's favour. Remember, when God opens a door, you walk through, you don't let nobody shut doors on you.

"I see you back in school doing some things, finishing some things that you started and God says this stage you got to compete because that's His next way of acceleration, leave nothing undone, reorganise, get things in order and finish what God has given you to do," Says the Lord.

"Leave nothing undone"

Recently, I have been reading the book of Joshua. God spoke so clearly to Joshua, I remember praying and asking God to speak to me with clarity the same way that He spoke to Joshua.

"As the Lord commanded Moses his servant, so did Moses command Joshua, and so did Joshua; he left nothing undone of all that the Lord commanded Moses." (Joshua 11:15).

That phrase 'leave nothing undone' stood out to me as I was able to draw a comparison. Joshua's testimony was that of accomplishing everything that he was supposed to do. God had already given me the same clear instructions before I even asked. *"He knows the things you have need of before you ask Him."* (Matthew 6:8)

When you find out what God wants you to do, "be strong and of good courage," God says *"I am with you wherever you go."* (Joshua 1:9)

I'm looking forward to the season of acceleration.

Conclusion

It takes faith to obtain the promises of God. One of my common trials in my Christian walk has been delay.

Sometimes God says that He will do something but He doesn't tell you exactly how or when it will come to pass. The devil can use this time to try and discourage you – I call it 'delay tactics'. The devil may have a plot, but God always has a plan! God is always faithful to His Word.

"So shall my Word be that springs forth from My mouth it shall not return to Me void, but it shall accomplish what I please and it shall prosper in the thing for which I sent it." (Isaiah 55:11)

If God said it then it will come to pass. Keep believing, keep trusting and keep fighting.

The Future belongs to those who see it beforehand.

The End

Printed in Great Britain
by Amazon

19104869R00071